Sister Girl
and the Training Wheels

Thank You,
Nicole F

By Nicole Fenner

Printed in the United States of America

ISBN : 13 : 978-0692812822
ISBN : 10 : 0692812822

Library of Congress Control Number : 2016920011
Sister Girl Publishing PO Box 811, Halifax, NC 27839

Sistergirlpublishing@gmail.com

Dedicated to the youth with eyes full of hope, works full of faith and hearts full of love. Continue to strive for excellence. In due time you will flourish into your ultimate self.

Love to my family, you have always guided me to the light and shielded me from the storm. I am forever grateful and appreciate you.

Sitting on the porch, smelling the sweet aroma of the beautiful rose bushes and listening to the buzzing bees flying around her head, Sister Girl watched the neighborhood children pedal down the street on their colorful bicycles, chattering, smiling, and laughing.

Sister Girl then thought of a wonderful idea. "I am going to learn how to ride a bike like a big kid all around town," she said out loud.

Sister Girl ran in the house and up to her dad sitting on the couch reading the newspaper.

"Daddy, I would like to learn how to ride a bike. Daddy, can you teach me?"

"Sister Girl, riding a bike is a great responsibility," replied Dad. "Are you ready for the challenge?"

"Yes, Daddy, I am ready for the challenge."

"You must remember that safety is key. Always wear a helmet when riding your bike. Pay attention to traffic, and be aware of pedestrians. I will teach you how to balance yourself and the bicycle."

Sister Girl was so excited to finally be a big kid. Dad and Sister Girl got in the car and went to town. On the way there Sister Girl told her dad that she wanted a sparkling red bike with a basket to hold her water bottle and her cat Jazzy.

Dad told Sister Girl, "We will see."

At the bicycle shop there were bikes of all types and sizes—single-speed, ten-speed, eighteen-speed, cruisers and mountain bikes.

The bikes were red, yellow, blue, and green. Sister Girl skipped all through the store, ponytail bouncing, and smiling from ear to ear.

She said with excitement in her voice, "Daddy! I found my bike!"

So, Dad walked to the back of the store and there it was—a red bike with splashes of pink, red handlebars, and a basket.

Sister Girl said, "Daddy, please can I have this bike?" Dad replied, "If this is the bike that you like, I will get it for you."

They went to the counter, and he paid for the bike.

On the drive home Sister Girl was the happiest little girl in the world. She was ready to ride to the park, to the library, and over to her friend's house.

After a ten-minute drive they arrived back home, and Dad took the bike out of the car.

Sister Girl was so eager that she jumped on the bike, and to her amazement she fell right to the ground.

Dad told Sister Girl, "You must first learn how to ride a bike. Like anything else, it takes time and practice. To learn how to read you have to sound out words. To count you have to learn your numbers. To learn a new language you must study."

Sister Girl stood up straight, dusted herself off, and with determination said, "I am ready to learn."

Dad walked with Sister Girl down the street to the neighborhood park.

Sister Girl felt proud. She was so excited to embark on this new adventure, and was so happy to share such a fun time with her Dad.

When they arrived at the park, Sister Girl fixed her helmet on her head.

Dad helped Sister Girl get on the bike. Sister Girl put her hands on the handlebars and her feet on the pedals.

Dad held on to the back of the bike seat to help guide Sister Girl around the park.

Sister Girl peddled and smiled, grinning and talking to Dad.

She said, "Dad, why are you holding on to the back of the bike? I am a big girl!"

Dad said, "I know, but I want to make sure my girl is safe."

Sister Girl smiled. "I get it, Dad."

After her first day at the park Sister Girl and Dad walked home. On their way they stopped at the ice cream shop for a Sunday evening dessert. Sister Girl got a vanilla cone with sprinkles, and Dad got a banana split.

The two sat in the shop eating their ice cream and talking about the next time Sister Girl would ride the bike.

ICE CREAM Stall

Dad told Sister Girl that he had a surprise for her and that she had to wait until Monday to see what it was. Sister Girl, being the anxious little girl that she was, asked Dad so many questions.

"What is the surprise, Dad? When will I get it—before school or after school?"

Dad smiled and said, "Just wait . . . it will be well worth it."

Sister Girl got ready for bed and went to sleep. The next morning she got up and went to school.

After school the big yellow bus dropped Sister Girl off at the end of the path. She skipped up the road to her house at the end of the street. While skipping up the road, she told her friends, "I will come and play with you later. My father has a surprise for me."

When Sister Girl arrived home, she washed her hands and sat at the kitchen table. Sister Girl ate her afternoon snack—a turkey sandwich, a pear, and a glass of water.

After her snack, she sat at her desk and completed her homework. Sister Girl then finished doing her chores with her sister.

Around six o'clock, Sister Girl heard a car arrive in the driveway. It was Dad. Sister Girl was so excited she jumped down the front steps of the house and did two cartwheels.

Sister Girl exclaimed, "Dad! I am ready for my surprise!"
Dad smiled and said, "Close your eyes."

So Sister Girl took her little hands and covered her eyes while peeking through her little fingers. After ten seconds Dad said, "Open your eyes!"

To Sister Girl's amazement, sitting in front of her was her bike! But now the bike had two additional wheels at the back.

Sister Girl, being the inquisitive little girl that she was, said, "All right, Dad. I am ready to be a big kid."
She got on the bike and to her amazement she could peddle on her own, and Dad did not have to hold the back of the bike.

Sister Girl peddled up and down the street. Her heart felt so warm and excited to ride her red bike in the neighborhood to see her friends. Sister Girl rode the bike the rest of the evening until she was tired and sleepy.

She came back to the yard and put the bike on the porch. Dad was sitting there by the rose bushes, and Sister Girl said, "Thanks, Dad, for teaching me how to ride a bike.
I never knew it took steps to ride a bike like a big kid."

Dad told Sister Girl that the training wheels would come off soon, but he wanted to make sure she was able to ride the bike on her own.

Sister Girl replied, "I am happy we took the steps. I am going to ride my bike until the training wheels fall off."